Signs All Around Us

Lorin Driggs

Signs are all around.
They keep us safe.

They show us where
to go.

What does this
sign mean?

It means restroom.

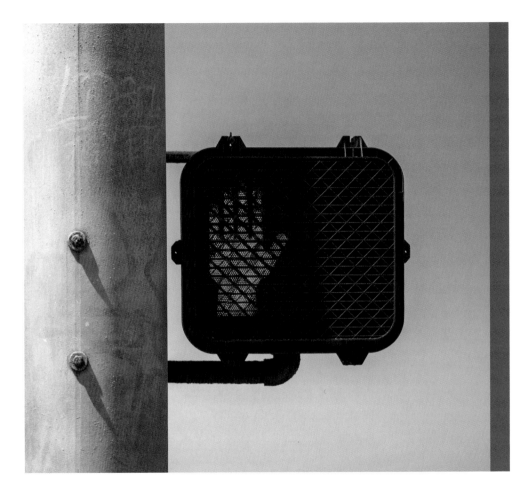

What does this sign mean?

It means don't walk.

What does this
sign mean?

It means walk.

What does this
sign mean?

It means trash can.

What does this
sign mean?

It means playground.

What does this
sign mean?

Think and Talk

Why do we need signs?

It means this is the place to vote.

Signs are all around!

Jump into Fiction

We Can Go!

Jen cannot use the stairs.

Where is the ramp?

There is a sign!

We can go to the show.

Civics in Action

Signs help us. They help us find things. They help us stay safe. They help us know which way to go.

1. Look at the signs around you.

2. Think about what else needs a sign.

3. Make your sign. Hang it up.